SHORT · SCENIC · WALKS

AIRE VALLEY

PAUL
HANNON

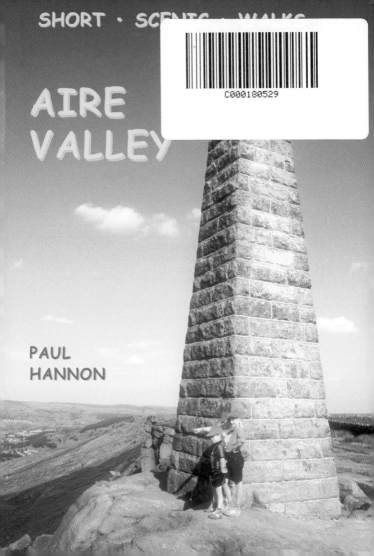

HILLSIDE PUBLICATIONS
20 Wheathead Crescent
Keighley
West Yorkshire
BD22 6LX

First Published 2008

© Paul Hannon 2008

ISBN 978 1 870141 87 1

The sketch maps are based on 1947 OS one-inch maps and earlier OS six-inch maps

Cover illustration: Leeds-Liverpool Canal under Farnhill Moor
Back cover: River Aire, Kildwick Bridge
Page 1: Wainman's Pinnacle, Earl Crag, Cowling
(Paul Hannon/Hillslides Picture Library)

Printed by Steffprint
Unit 5, Keighley Industrial Park
Royd Ings Avenue
Keighley
West Yorkshire
BD21 4DZ

CONTENTS

INTRODUCTION

On leaving the Yorkshire Dales National Park the still youthful River Aire begins a remarkably fascinating course down through the Pennine moors. The Aire Valley is populated by towns of substantial size such as Keighley, Bingley and Shipley, yet everywhere it reveals features of immense character and interest. A score of part rural, part commuter villages such as Cononley, Bradley, Cowling and East Morton are sprinkled at regular intervals along the valley, while a little more off the beaten track are gems such as Micklethwaite and Lothersdale. Between the buzzing market town of Skipton and the world heritage site of Saltaire, the Aire winds a largely unfrequented course along the valley floor, paralleled by the more trafficked and colourful Leeds & Liverpool Canal. Hilly flanks rise on either side to the ever popular local landmarks of Earl Crag, Farnhill Moor, Shipley Glen and the Druid's Altar: lesser known scenic corners include Holden Beck, Sunnydale, Ramshaw and the Doubler Stones. Such a well-frequented area has much of man's work on show too, notably the likes of the Five Rise Locks, Cononley Lead Mine and Saltaire.

A feature of the area is its accessibility from nearby towns and cities, notably the West Yorkshire giants of Bradford and Leeds: proof you needn't travel far to enjoy delightful walking in absorbing surroundings. Most walks are served by public transport, with trains and buses linking Keighley, midway, with Saltaire, Skipton and the villages in between. Whilst the route description should be sufficient to guide you around, a map is recommended for greater information: Ordnance Survey 1:25,000 scale maps give the best detail, and Explorers OL21 and 288 cover all but one of the walks, along with Explorer 297.

Micklethwaite

USEFUL INFORMATION

·Skipton Tourist Information (01756-792809)
·Haworth Tourist Information (01535-642329)
·Bradford Tourist Information (01274-433678)
·Ramblers' Association, 2nd Floor, Camelford House, 87-89 Albert Embankment, London SE1 7BR (020-7339 8500)
·Traveline - public transport information (0870-6082608)

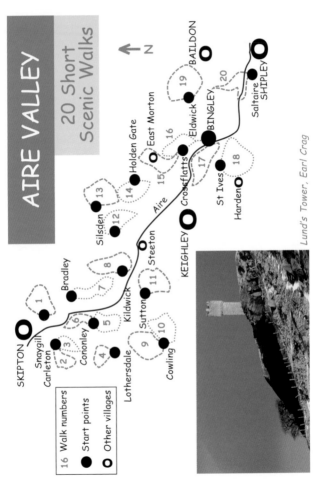

AIRE VALLEY

20 Short Scenic Walks

← N

Lund's Tower, Earl Crag

SKIPTON

1

Snaygill
Carleton

2 3 6
Cononley

Bradley

4

7 8

5

Kildwick

Lothersdale

Sutton 11

9 10

Cowling

Silsden

13

12

14

Holden Gate

Aire

Steeton

KEIGHLEY

Crossflatts

15 16

East Morton

19

BAILDON

Eldwick

BINGLEY

17

20

St Ives 18

Harden

Saltaire
SHIPLEY

16	Walk numbers
●	Start points
○	Other villages

6

A RECORD OF YOUR WALKS

WALK	DATE	NOTES
1		
2		
3		
4		
5		
6		
7		
8		
9		
10		
11	11.2.21	Nice wood w/stream; views; 30 min. drive
12		
13		
14		
15		
16		
17		
18		
19		
20		

*4 miles
from Snaygill*

**A grand climb to open
country with magnificent
views from the Aire Valley
high into the Dales**

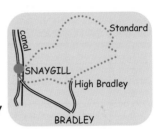

*Start Low Snaygill (GR: 992497), lay-by opposite large hotel
Map OS Explorer OL21, South Pennines*

Join the Leeds-Liverpool Canal at Snaygill swing bridge behind the large hotel, and turn right on the towpath. Passing the Bay Horse pub you reach Snaygill Bridge, but without passing under step up onto the road, and across the bridge take a farm drive on the left. From a stile on its right slant up a field to a wall, where a farm track rises to a gate. Already you have big views up Airedale to the Malhamdale fells, Flasby Fell and Crookrise Crag. Unlike the track, pass through and slant left to the ascending wall. After a bend slant left again to rejoin the wallside track, still ascending. Part way up is a stile in it: don't pass through, instead cross to a wall-stile opposite, beneath a stony bank. Head away with a wall on your left to quickly reach another stile onto a grassy lane. This brings a big view down the Aire Valley. Turn left along its inviting course to rise to a gate onto the access road serving High Bradley.

This climbs out of the hamlet to swing right as a farm drive rising across fields. As it turns down to New House, go straight on a grassy way to a gate ahead. Maintain this course to the next gateway, then as it forks take the left branch to a gate ahead. By now you have massive views back over the Aire Valley to the South Pennines, featuring Boulsworth Hill and Pinhaw, with Parlick's cone on the distant Bowland moors. Making use of Open Access, don't pass through but rise left with the wall to a gate. From it a grassy way slants left up into bracken. Reaching a wall on the brow, bear right on a trod running to the boulders on Millstone Hill.

This reveals the highest point of the Standard across Black Sike. Waymarks send a path on a bee-line for a wall-corner across the marsh, evading its excesses by crossing the outflow. When a wall comes up from the left, easier going brings arrival at a stile in the corner, on the Standard. This stunning moment earns a fine prospect of the Aire Gap, and a bird's-eye view of Skipton: beyond, the hills of Craven include Flasby Fell, Crookrise Crag and Barden Moor. A grand little path traces a sunken way down in the Skipton direction. Beyond the head of a marshy area, an obvious fork left leads to a stile by a wall corner. Just to the right the path continues down, and when this forks at a few reeds, again bear left, a grassy way slanting back to the wall to reach a stile in it just short of a wall corner. From it bear gently away from the wall, a broad grass track passing above boulders before dropping to a gate/stile in a wall below. Slant left down the field (woodland on the map!) to find a stile just above a gate in the bottom corner.

Entering wooded Cawder Gill turn down the near side, a track forming to drop to a gate/stile into a field. Advance past a wall corner to a track just short of Cawder Hall, and go down this to the main drive. A little further down it, level with Horse Close, pass through a small gate on the left to a stile behind. Bear right down the field centre, over the base of a knoll to find a wall-stile. A path shadows a hummocky crest to squeeze through a snicket in the bottom corner onto a lane back at Snaygill swing bridge.

The Standard from Millstone Hill

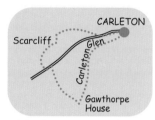

$3^1 4$ miles
from Carleton

**A pleasant contrast
between wooded beckside
and open country
overlooking the Aire Gap**

Start Village centre (GR: 972496), roadside parking
Map OS Explorer OL21, South Pennines

Grouped around the large former mill are the Swan Inn, church, Post office and shop. From the pub head west on the Colne road past the mill, and just before the last house on the left turn on The Wend. After swinging round to the right follow it as it bridges Catlow Gill and swings right to run parallel with it. Beyond assorted farm buildings it emerges to run as a lovely grass track through several fields, with the tree-lined beck down to the right. Reaching a pronounced bend in the beck, the track fades at a gate: through it a thin path turns upstream on the rim of the steep-sided gill. Part way up the field it becomes apparent you're now above a side beck, and a marker post sends a faint path slanting into the floor of the gill. Cross a stile and then the stream, and a path winds up the opposite bank. Directly in front of you is the well-defined ditch of a circular ancient enclosure sloped across the field. There is a first glimpse of Ingleborough across the southern Dales.

Resume left atop the bank and up to a wall-stile ahead. Looking back, the expanse of Barden Moor rises behind Skipton, with Kirkby Fell, Fountains Fell and Great Whernside further up the Dales. Slant right up a large field to a gate at the top, on the rim of Carleton Glen. Through this, contour across and then a path forms to drop to the beck in an obvious gap in the trees. Across, go a few yards up to a stile in a short length of wall. Climb away again and resume left above the bank, again to a wall-stile ahead. From this aim directly up the field to Gawthorpe House above, join-ing its drive at a stile. Turn right on the driveway which winds its way down onto a road. This stretch gives ample time to enjoy the sweeping panorama: Ingleborough is joined by the top of Penyghent, while Great Whernside is joined by Buckden Pike above the cleft of Flasby Fell. Go left up the road for 100 yards to a bridle-gate on the right, from where a thin path heads away with a wall onto the heather moorland of Scarcliff. On the brow, before the end of the wall, the path swings away from it and curves to the right, winding down the moor to the house at Higher Scarcliff.

Follow the drive along the moorfoot until level with Lower Scarcliff, and turn left to pass right of the house to a concrete drive behind. Bear left on this across to a cattle-grid in the wall, and just a little further double back right to find a stile in the wall you just passed through. Cross a tree-lined trickle and along the top of new plantings to a wall-stile at the end. Now begins a crossing of several fields, largely in a straight line with wall-stiles in place. At the end you drop to one alongside a duckpond: here take a fence-stile behind and resume alongside a fence to the end. Ignore the track in favour of a wall-stile in front, and advance to the next gate/stile in front of Sixpenny Syke Farm. Just behind take a gate on the right and along the house side to rejoin the road. Turn left for a few minutes return into Carleton.

Flasby Fell across the Aire Gap from Scarcliff

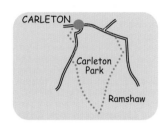

CARLETON

Carleton
Park

Ramshaw

*2³⁄₄ miles
from Carleton*

**A short ascent leads
to an outstanding
moorland viewpoint**

Start **Village centre (GR: 972496), roadside parking**
Map **OS Explorer OL21, South Pennines**

Grouped around the large former mill are the Swan Inn,
church, Post office and shop. From the pub head west on the Colne
road alongside the mill, and at the end take a grassy snicket on the
left, alongside a wooded beck. When the beck swings right climb
straight ahead up steps into new housing. Cross straight over and
up between houses to a small gate into a big sloping field. Ascend
straight up, looking back on super views over the village to Skipton
and into the Dales. Rising past a wall corner, the going eases at a
crumbling wall, where bear left to a stile in a wall onto a road.

Turn right, gently uphill, and after levelling out go left to
a gate set back: don't pass through but take a little gate on the
right, and ascend an enclosure with the wall on your left. At the top
corner is a stile into a field: Ramshaw waits ahead. Slant across to
a corner gate, then continue to the wall ahead and bear right with
it to a corner gate/stile into Carleton Park Farm. Pass a pond and
over a plank bridge to the drive, and with the house on the left go
straight ahead to a gate by a cattle-grid. Follow the wall away,
ignoring a drive which cuts back to the wall, and when the wall turns
off advance to two gates in the wall ahead. In the kink between, a
wall-stile admits into the rough pasture of Ramshaw. A grassy
track ascends the wallside, easing out to meet a wall corner on the
ridge. New views ahead look over the Aire Valley to Rombalds Moor.

Don't use the gate but turn left on a thin trod along the
moorland crest of Ramshaw. This narrows a little to give better

airy views before reaching the abrupt start of the descent. This high, broad ridge with its delightful heathery top gives sweeping views: countless Airedale villages and landmarks can be picked out, while beyond rise the Bowland moors, Ingleborough, Malhamdale hills, Fountains Fell, Flasby Fell, Buckden Pike, Great Whernside, Barden Moor, Simon's Seat, Skipton Moor, Beamsley Beacon and Rombalds Moor. Drop off the end through newly planted trees and down to a corner stile. Remain with the wall through a couple of gates, by-passing Carleton Biggin to a wall-stile just below it: this sends an enclosed path onto its drive. Turn left down it, and with a road just ahead, take stiles in the adjacent fence and wall to cross the field to a similar stile. From here descend to a fence-stile to drop down a few steps onto a track at the barns of Carla Beck Farm. Go briefly left to drop down a short track onto a road.

Turn left along the footway to re-enter the village. On the left is Spence's Court, 17th century almshouses with spinning galleries above a courtyard. To vary the finish bear right between houses opposite, a flagged path running on to St Mary's church. A continuation high-walled snicket runs on to emerge by the Post office. The Swan is just to the left, or to finish with a little more of the village, go briefly right on Church Street then bear left on a rough road before the bridge. This traces the beck upstream, outside the mill at the end to re-emerge onto the Colne road.

Descending from Ramshaw

*3 miles
from Lothersdale*

**A short, easy route
from a secluded village
onto a popular local
moorland landmark**

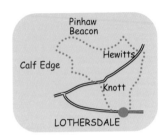

Start Village centre (GR: 959459), roadside parking
Map OS Explorer OL21, South Pennines

Lothersdale is a highly attractive village strung along a quiet back road, well off the beaten track. Being hidden among folds of the hills did not prevent the arrival of the mill age, and the surviving chimney is often all that can be seen of the village. The church stands high and isolated to the east, while other features - including a limestone quarry that has unearthed prehistoric bones - are found further west. From the Hare & Hounds pub head east on the main street for a matter of yards, and take the Pennine Way signed up through a farmyard. An enclosed track climbs to emerge into a field. Ascend the wallside with a wooded stream over to the right, all the way up to a stile at the top corner. Go left up the field to a stile/gate onto a road. Cross over and up Hewitts farm road. When it goes left keep straight up an enclosed grassy way into a field, then up the wallside to a stile onto a corner of Elslack Moor.

A well-worn path remains with the wall until breaking free to rise to Pinhaw. Within 300 yards of the top a stone sees a grooved path double back right, its fading course running 130 yards down to a small inscribed stone marked on the map. Robert Wilson died here in 1805, one of the guards who manned the beacon: men of three surrounding parishes shared the duties. The broad path runs on to the OS column and cairn on Pinhaw. At 1273ft/388m it boasts an extensive 360-degree panorama, with the Dales fells to the north being finest feature: keen eyes might pick out the limestone cliff of Malham Cove. The summit is distinguishable as the raised site of a beacon, one of a long chain that stretched across the country centuries ago, and lit to warn of impending danger and also celebrate major events.

Two paths leave, but merge within 100 yards amid Elslack Moor's heathery knolls. A wall corner is quickly reached and the PW is finally left. Go left with the wall, and beyond a small marsh a good little path runs over the brow. This gives a fine view over the dale, with the old limestone quarry at Raygill prominent, along with parts of the scattered village with the mill chimney conspicuous. The path curves left above a wall corner and along to a solid stile off the moor. Bear left, down past a wood corner and across a field to a gate/stile at the bottom. Descend the wallside to a stile onto a drive at Calf Edge. Go left on this which runs on and down onto a road.

Go left for two minutes along the road, and over a stream turn right down a drive to The Knott, a fine house of some age. Go straight on down a short track in front of it, then from the left-hand gate a grassy track runs on between wall and fence. At the end it swings right to a gate in the corner. Head straight down the wallside, with the village millpond below. At the bottom corner ignore a gate in favour of a wall-stile in front. Drop to another stile and a bridge over the outflow onto the road. Go left to finish.

Lothersdale, with Earl Crag beyond

5 ━━━ CONONLEY LEAD MINE

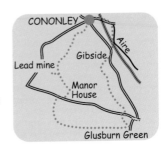

*4 miles
from Cononley*

**A simple circuit of
Cononley's own hill, with
the unique attraction
of an old lead mine**

Start Village centre (GR: 989469), car park on Moorfoot
Lane, where Meadow Lane leaves Main Street
Map OS Explorer OL21, South Pennines

Head up Main Street past the New Inn, and leave by an
access road on the near side of the Institute. It climbs steeply
towards Town Head Farm, but is left at the sharp bend just before
it, instead continuing straight up a walled green way. At the top
turn right with a gradually rising wall on an improving grassy track.
Good views look back over the village, up the Aire Valley. The way
runs to houses, Great and Little Gib. Advance on the access road,
noting a wall-stile on the left opposite the second house: you will
resume from here. For the lead mine follow the drive around the
corner. The restored workings at Yorkshire's southernmost lead
mine are dominated by a chimney and a Cornish-style engine house.
The buildings date from around 1842, and though mining ceased in
1882, the spoil was worked for barytes during the 20th century.

Back at the stile slant right up the large field, tracing
the wall to a stile. Heading away, a track forms to lead through a
gateway and along a wallside to Manor House Farm. Pass along the
rear of the house and out on the drive onto Lothersdale Road. Turn
briefly right then go left on an access road. Follow the track down
fieldsides, with Cowling village beneath its landmarks on Earl Crag
ahead. Faced with two gates the track goes right: you take the left
gate to slant down to a wall-stile along the bottom. Drop down a
wallside to the houses at West Closes, where gates lead through an

enclosure and down a house side. Go left along the front and out on its access road, which runs pleasantly on and then past several farms almost to its emergence onto Green Lane at Glusburn Green.

Leave it, however, just before the end, where a driveway doubles back left over a cattle-grid to Buckett Farm. Pass along the front to a stile, then up through a gate and ascend the field as far as a stile in the adjacent wall. Cross this and a stile behind, then slant up the field to a gate left of buildings at Well Spring Farm. Succeeding gates put you back onto Lothersdale Road. Turn right past the farm, after which take a wallside track leaving a gate on the left. As it fades keep on to the end to a kissing-gate and advance past an old reservoir to emerge into the open. Extensive Aire Valley views feature Rombalds, Farnhill and Skipton Moors, while behind Skipton rise shapely Flasby Fell and also Barden Moor.

The path runs on though an old stile and slants down to a gate to merge into an old grassy track on a hairpin bend. This angles gently down to a gate. Through it a farm track is met above Gibside. Turn down this through a gate, and it winds down to join the drive of the house. Follow this down to the road and go left for 100 yards. From a ladder-stile on the right cross the railway line with care and a path makes a pleasant short stroll with the River Aire. An iron kissing-gate takes the path through greenery to emerge by the road bridge. Turn left on the footway alongside the beck back into the village via the level crossing.

Cononley Lead Mine

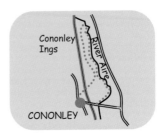

*4½ miles from
Cononley*

**A leisurely ramble clinging
to the winding banks of
the Aire: hills all around
but this is dead flat!**

*Start Village centre (GR: 989469), car park on Moorfoot
Lane, where Meadow Lane leaves Main Street
Map OS Explorer OL21, South Pennines
Access After heavy rain the fields can become seriously
flooded: in normal conditions there are no problems*

Cononley is a traditional Airedale mill village. Its centre
hides many attractive old cottages, a Post office/shop and two
pubs, the New Inn and the Railway. It also has a railway station,
though its level crossing causes the road to be closed as much as it
is open! Head east along the street, in tandem with the beck across
the level crossing and out of the village on a footway. Reaching a
bridge on the River Aire, take a stile and stone steps on the left
sending a path heading upstream.

Here begins an extended riverbank ramble that adheres
tightly to the Aire around innumerable twists and turns. Kissing-
gates and later stiles are the only interruptions on this lovely
grassy bank, mostly with a flood embankment alongside. Across
the valley Farnhill Moor sits above its woods, while above the village of
Bradley rise the slopes of the Standard culminating on the crest of
Skipton Moor. Ahead, the much vaster girth of Barden Moor rises
beyond Skipton, with Crookrise Crag and later Embsay Crag as its
prominent features. A delightful walk clings faithfully for over two
miles until a sharp bend just short of a low railway bridge across
the river.

Don't advance any further but double sharply back left across the field centre, locating a stile in the fence some distance ahead (with a gate further to its left). This very flat no-man's-land of Cononley Ings is indeed an interesting vantage point for the comprehensive, contrasting surround of Aire Valley hills! Maintain this line over two further stiles and across a ditch and a large embankment, then straight on again over a cross-track to reach a small wooden footbridge on a deep drain. From a stile behind this bear left with the drain on your left. This abandoned stretch of water known as Dead Eye makes a good wildlife habitat: swans are often seen among the reeds.

Reaching a stile in a tumbledown section of wall, a clear path runs through this scrub alongside Dead Eye. Over a wall-stile at the end advance on with the fence and bank on your left to a sturdy footbridge on a drain in the tapering corner. From a stile a few yards to the left, bear right to one in the hedgerow just ahead. This admits onto Shady Lane. Turn right on this hedgerowed track which leads unfailingly back to the village, exercising caution at a level crossing en route. Joining Skipton Road go left for the village centre, either on to Main Street at the end, or turning left on Meadow Lane for the car park.

A flooded River Aire at Cononley Ings, Ramshaw behind

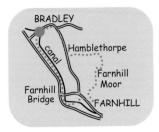

*3½ miles
from Bradley*

**The heathery delights of
one of Airedale's best
locations are reached by
a lovely canalside stroll**

Start **Ings Lane, by canal (GR: 000482), car park**
Map **OS Explorer OL21, South Pennines**

From the car park cross the canal bridge and turn left
on the towpath. Within half a mile you pass Hamblethorpe swing
bridge: a memorial recalls seven Polish airmen whose Wellington
bomber perished nearby in 1943. The towpath leads on towards
Farnhill, notable features being Farnhill Woods with its awesome
bluebell carpet, Farnhill Bridge with its view up to the Pinnacle, a
canal milestone, and the dark turrets of Farnhill Hall peering
through trees across a loop of the canal. Just past this comes the
next swing bridge, crossing this one to leave the canal. Through a
wall-stile opposite turn briefly right along the bank to an old iron
kissing-gate, then curve left up the field to a small gate in the wall
at the top. Joining a drive curve briefly up it but then take a tall,
slim gate above to emerge onto a road on the edge of Farnhill.

Turn briefly right along the footway, then as the road
prepares to fork take a kissing-gate set back on the left just up a
driveway. An enclosed path rises to the base of a wood. Keep right
as it forks, running on through trees to join a broad path. Double
back left here, gradually narrowing and emerging from trees onto
the base of Farnhill Moor. Ignoring any branches remain on this
fine path as it curves up to the right past an old quarry to meet a
path at right-angles in front of Crag Top farm. Turn left on this,
passing through a gateway to enter the main body of the moor.
Immediately forking at a seat, take the left one rising gently on

20

and up through bracken and increasing heather and gritstone slabs to only reveal the Jubilee Tower as you're almost upon it.

Locally known as Farnhill Pinnacle, this prominent 12ft high monument was erected in 1887 to commemorate the Golden Jubilee of Queen Victoria. Words carved on an adjacent stone explain that it was restored on the occasion of the Silver Jubilee of King George V in 1935. Alongside is a seat from which to survey the Airedale vista. Across the valley is Cononley, while meandering below is a good length of the canal: down-dale Earl Crag and its monuments patrol the skyline, while beyond Skipton are the peaks of Flasby Fell.

From the pinnacle go to the path crossroads a few yards east, and continue inland directly away to rise gently to a large cairn that soon appears. Here turn sharp left on a clear little path that runs north, passing a stone shelter to reach the wall ahead, curving left to a seat there. Over the wall, a big pile of stones in the heather is an ancient burial mound. Turning left, a thinner but good path remains with the wall all the way down to the road. Go right for a few level minutes to old Hamblethorpe Farm, and Bradley appears below, backed by the Standard. All that remains is a steep descent down into the village to finish, bearing left after the Slaters Arms to reach the canal via sports fields.

On Farnhill Moor

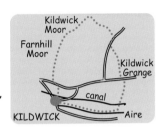

*4 miles
from Kildwick*

**Outstanding features of
interest range from moor,
river and canal to fine
architectural highlights**

*Start Village centre (GR: 010458), roadside parking
Map OS Explorer OL21, South Pennines*

Kildwick presents a delightful scene: the White Lion pub overlooks the graceful old bridge, backed by beautiful St Andrew's church. Within are 10th century cross remains and the de Styveton monument of 1307. Take the road up the side of the church, going right past the old school of 1839. Across Parson's Bridge on the Leeds-Liverpool Canal a flagged snicket rises through greenery to emerge into a field, continuing up to a road. Worth seeing just to the right is Kildwick Hall, a magnificent 17th century manor house.

The route goes left a short way: opposite Starkey Lane a path goes right through a kissing-gate to the edge of a sliver of moorland. Rising into open surrounds, it curves away from the wall to look over the valley to Cononley. Above a short-lived quarry edge the path passes the houses at Crag Top to a gateway onto the main tract of Farnhill Moor. Within yards the path forks: take the right branch rising away, remaining near a wall on the right as it ascends the moor edge, through heather, bracken and scrub. Towards the end of a stand of silver birch is a path crossroads. Take a thinner one right, rising through scattered trees to a wall-stile onto Kildwick Moor. A path bears left, leaving bracken for rough grass with views to Flasby Fell and the Malhamdale hills. From a stile in the very corner, cross the field to one in the facing wall, then go right to shadow the wall to a stile at the end. Keep on to a stile behind a small copse, then cross beyond the wood to cut a corner to a stile. Across the field centre is a gate beneath another small wood, this time passing to its right. Continue beyond it to a gate at the end, then along a short green track to a stile onto New Lane.

Turn right past the house at Great Slack to a barn just beyond. From a stile on the left drop past the barn and bear right to a wall-stile. Continue down to a fence-stile below, and maintain the line down to a stile in the bottom corner. Now bear right with the wall down to find a wall-stile in the very bottom corner (boundary stone at its foot). From this cross to a stile in the wall across, onto a grassy walled way. Turn down this, soon joining the stream, becoming a track to descend into the exclusive hamlet of Kildwick Grange. Remain on the access road which runs down onto a road. The last house on the right is Grange Farm, with mullioned windows.

Turn left a short way then take a gate on the right and descend a grassy track, all the way down the fields to cross a swing bridge on the canal. For the quickest finish go right on the towpath for a few minutes' walk back into Kildwick. For a conclusion with the River Aire, go straight on the enclosed path from a gate opposite, descending between old walls. Emerging, continue down to a gate at the bottom. Turn right through this and along the fence to a stile at the end, with the river just in front. Turn right to another stile and head off on a grassy embankment above the river. This leads unfailingly along to Kildwick Bridge, joining the road by a stile.

Kildwick church

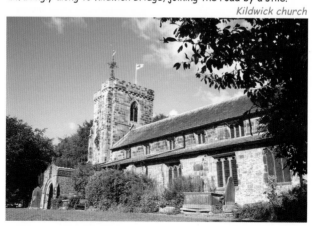

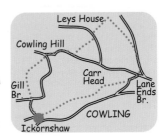

*4¾ miles
from Cowling*

**An absorbing exploration
of the richly varied
country between
Cowling and Lothersdale**

*Start **Ickornshaw (GR: 967430)** off main road at
western end of village, roadside parking by church
Map OS Explorer OL21, South Pennines*

Cowling is a windswept gritstone mill community, indeed a classic Pennine example. Its rows of dark terraces including the Bay Horse pub are strung along the length of the village on the main road over to Lancashire. The 19th century church of the Holy Trinity stands aloof: from a gate to its right head away on an access track. Cowling village is strung beneath the pinnacled escarpment of Earl Crag. The track runs on to end at a barn. Take the right-hand of two gates behind a kissing-gate, and a splendid path runs along the wooded bank top of Ickornshaw Beck to a path junction at isolated Wood House. Bear left to drop down to cross the parallel Gill Beck on Ridge Mill footbridge. Resume downstream on the bank of this new beck, a super path that leads all the way to a high wooden footbridge onto a road. En route you pass a fine old limekiln as you enter the park-like surrounds of Carr Head.

Go left to cross the road bridge and up to a junction just above. Opposite, a couple of yards left is a gap-stile, and stone steps send a little path down the bank to a stile onto a road at another bridge. Cross and take the road climbing away as far as Leys Laithe on the left. From a wall-stile above it slant up to a wall corner to commence a splendid stride along the wallside high above the valley of Leys Beck. After two fields you alight onto an access road at Leys House. Turn left down an inviting, grassy walled way, slanting down at the bottom to a ford and footbridge on Leys Beck. Across, a firm path ascends through deep foliage onto a minor road. Cross and resume on a continuing way, initially still deep within greenery, and making a more sustained pull before opening out as a track to join another back road. Turn right for a few minutes' final pull to the farming hamlet of Cowling Hill.

At the junction rise right past Cowling Hill Farm to a bend at the entrance to a burial ground. Go left, descending into the concrete yard and noting the Baptist Chapel (founded 1744) on your left. Pass through a gate and down to the bottom, where the right-hand gate at the last barn sends a grassy walled way off. The big view ahead looks over the Cowling scene to Earl Crag, Ickornshaw Moor and Boulsworth Hill. The way swings round to emerge into a field. A fainter track advances along the fieldtop to a gate/stile at the end. Don't pass through but turn down the wall-side, a faint path dropping to a gate/stile below. With the old farm at Low Stubbing to the left, drop straight down to a slim gap-stile in the hedge below, then down colourful slopes to a wall-stile at the bottom. Down again, a long-drained dam and gateway precede a kissing-gate sending you left on a short-lived enclosed path onto a grassy driveway. Advance on this to emerge onto a back road at Gill Bridge. Cross and ascend to a junction with Gill Lane, which follow left back to the start, passing the long terrace of Middleton.

In the valley of Leys Beck

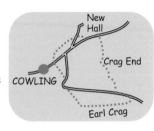

New Hall

Crag End

COWLING

Earl Crag

*3¹4 miles
from Cowling*

**Airedale's finest gritstone
escarpment supports two
local landmarks and gives
breathtaking views**

Start Village centre (GR: 974433), roadside parking
Map OS Explorer OL21, South Pennines

Head east (Keighley-bound) along the street, and near
the end turn right up the suburban Collinge Road. At the top left
corner a snicket slants up to a field. A flagged path climbs away,
slanting more faintly left to a kissing-gate at the top. This admits
to the drive of Crag Side: go left the few yards onto a road.
Wainman's Pinnacle on Earl Crag hovers above. Rise a short way to
a sharp bend then take an old gate onto the foot of the moor. A
clear path rises away, bound for the monument. Though several
ways branch off (including a very early fork, where keep left) and
numerous sunken ways are encountered, this same path climbs
through colourful vegetation to the rocks beneath the pinnacle, the
final section as a well engineered old green way. Clamber through
the modest rocks to gain the edge path, and thence the pinnacle.

Earl Crag is a mile-long gritstone edge which dominates
the South Craven skyline. Atop it, a long half-mile apart, are its two
occupants, with Lund's Tower now revealed at the far end. Built on
solid rock, the pinnacle dates from the early 19th century. The
panorama includes Farnhill Moor, Pinhaw Beacon, Flasby Fell,
Barden Moor, Skipton Moor, Rombalds Moor and villages such as
Cross Hills, Bradley and Kildwick. The promenade along the crest of
Earl Crag to the Tower is as obvious as it looks, encountering two
kissing-gates and finally a stile in a fence. Set back from an old
quarry, the tower boasts 39 dark, spiral steps to a platform from
which to survey the exhilarating vista far into the Yorkshire Dales.

Leave by a path from the fence, which circumvents the cliff on steps down towards the road. Turn left down this as far as a drive to Brush on the right. Earl Crag now presents a jagged sky-line above. Ignoring the drive descend left to a gate, below which is a short enclosed way. At the bottom follow the wall down through one further field, and through the stile take another on your left. Slant across to the bottom corner then cross to Crag End ahead. Joining its drive at the entrance, double back right down it to descend through fields, and ultimately enclosed onto the main road.

Cross to the footway and turn left as far as the first drive, New Hall Farm. Drop down to the cobbled yard in front of the main house and go left. Facing you is a wall-stile into a field. Follow a hedge away to Lane Ends Farm, passing through the yard to emerge onto a back road. Go left, and after Middle Lane Ends Farm take a gate set back on the right. From a stile behind it ascend the hedgeside, through a kissing-gate at the top and up again, with a wall on the right through two further fields. From a wall-stile advance with a wall enclosing sports fields on your left, and a colourful valley on your right. Passing an outdoor centre to reach a gate at the tapering corner, pass through an old farmyard and then left up the access road to re-enter the village.

Ascending to Earl Crag

*4½ miles
from Sutton-in-Craven*

**A hugely colourful walk
sees richly wooded
cloughs give way to
excellent views**

Start Village centre (GR: 005441), roadside parking
Map OS Explorer OL21, South Pennines

Sutton is a thriving village with three pubs and several shops. From the main junction outside the park and the Black Bull follow High Street left. Keep left to a fork just before the beck, and take unsigned Hall Drive ahead. This suburban street runs beneath the arch of a double lodge, and at the end a footbridge takes a broad path into wooded Sutton Clough. Keep on the main way, passing arched bridge, footbridge and concrete bridge before crossing a small footbridge. A path traces the opposite bank to a beautiful confluence, then begins to climb. Enjoy lovely waterplay as the often muddy path climbs between boulders. The path stays near the beck until it turns to climb steeply and more firmly away. Here leave it, and advance a few yards to the stream to cross to the opposite bank. A few yards upstream a good path doubles back up the slope to the left to a stile out of the clough.

Turn right up to a house: from a corner stile an enclosed path curves left outside the grounds to a ladder-stile by a stone outhouse. The first of the open views looks updale to Farnhill Moor and beyond. Descend the wallside to a stile into a stream's wooded confines: a waterfall tumbles over a rocky ledge below. Within fifty yards a less obvious, part-stepped path drops down to cross the beck, and on a short way to a stile out. Contour round the sloping field to an interesting stile above the trees of another branch of the clough. Negotiate rampant hollies to a hidden stile at the top, then shadow a wall up to neighbouring stiles onto an access road. Go left through the farm and out to a road. Cross over to Long House, behind which a walled way leads into a field. Massive views include Sutton Clough, Cowling Tower, the Malhamdale hills, Fountains Fell, Flasby Fell and Barden Moor. Cross to a gate, then pass beneath a stone hut to a stile ahead. Advance into bracken to a corner stile, then go left to a gate into Valley Farm's yard. Pass through and out on a walled way. Emerging into a field cross to a stile right of two masts, then on to bridle-gates through a sliver of trees. Head on through an old gateway then bear right to a gate onto a drive.

Head along the drive until just before a bend, then take a gate on the left from where a grassy track drops away. To the left is the stony edge of Eastburn Crag. An enclosed section leads down to colourful country around an old quarry. The grand path slants down well above the quarry, and as it curves down the side, a short-cut drops directly down. The track becomes an access road dropping into Eastburn as Moor Lane by the Post office: further left is the Eastburn Inn. Cross the main road and go left down Green Lane. At the bottom turn left on Lyon Road to rejoin the main road. Cross and go right, leaving by a surfaced path after crossing Holme Beck at Eastburn Bridge. Ahead is the Earl Crag skyline. This firm path shadows the beck all the way to Sutton, ignoring a footbridge part way along. Rejoining the road, turn left and conclude through the park.

Looking across Sutton Clough

—12— SWARTHA & BRUNTHWAITE

*3½ miles
from Silsden*

**Easy rambling by towpath,
fields and hamlets fringing
a bustling little town**

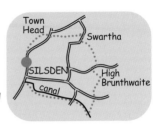

Start Town centre (GR: 041464), car parks
Map OS Explorer OL21, South Pennines

Head south along the main street (Kirkgate) and cross
the canal bridge to descend stone steps alongside the Bridge Inn.
Joining the towpath of the Leeds-Liverpool Canal, head east out of
town. Modern housing developments on the opposite bank finally
end and open fields look across the valley, with Spring Crag Wood
ahead. Crossing a narrow lane at Brunthwaite swing bridge, advance
to Holden Bridge. This swing bridge sends a walled track to Howden
Grange and Howden Park Farms, out through the yard onto Holden
Lane. Go left over the bridge and leave by a gate up to the right.
Slant up the field to a stile by the top corner, and up again to one
to the right. A short-lived enclosed way runs out to a stile onto an
access road bend. Turn right up this where it ends at a house, and
instead pass through a gap on the left to enter Silsden golf course.

Head away with the wall, which turns off to leave you
heading across the centre of the course guided by green and white
posts. A straight line leads on towards the edge, passing right of
some final shrubbery to a wall. Pass through a small gate into the
enclosure in front, and with a gate midway, cross to a stile onto a
back road at High Brunthwaite. Turn uphill to a bend, then take a
gate on the left to pass beneath farm buildings, curving round at
the end and up through the extensive, ramshackle yard to a gate
at the far corner, then around to leave by another gate to the left.
The grassy track quickly fades in the field, leaving you to cross to
a stile in the wall ahead. Big views look over to South Craven under

Earl Crag. Entering trees a nice path runs up to a footbridge on Brunthwaite Beck. Downstream is a surprisingly tall double-arched stone aqueduct, carrying water from the Barden Moor reservoirs to Bradford. Downstream is a small series of falls. Up the other side ignore a stile in front and go left on the wood-top path, splendidly along to a wall-stile out of the trees, with a Bradford Corporation Waterworks stone of 1858 alongside. The path then runs on above undergrowth to Swartha House Farm and out onto a road.

Turn uphill, again briefly, to the hamlet of Swartha. At the first chance pass through a kissing-gate on the left and along beneath a house to a minor brow revealing a super view over Silsden. Dropping down, a green way forms to curve left down alongside a wall enclosing a new wood. At the bottom corner a little gate and stile admit onto a steeply descending walled snicket. At the bottom squeeze through a gap-stile in front and resume down the hedgeside, through a gap-stile at the bottom and down again to another corner one. The now enclosed grassy path swings right to descend past a set of allotments to emerge onto Bolton Road on the edge of Silsden. Cross to the footway and go a few yards right to a stile. Then cross the fieldside to another onto a back lane at Town Head. Go left and descend all the way back into the centre, passing some nice old cottages with mullioned windows.

Looking over Silsden to Earl Crag

*3½ miles
from Silsden*

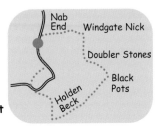

**A colourful side valley
and iconic gritstone
landmarks lead to a
stunning moorland viewpoint**

Start Lightbank Lane (GR: 062470), lay-bys on summit of
road reached from Town Head, Silsden by Brownbank Lane
Map OS Explorer OL21, South Pennines (or 297)

From the outset enjoy outstanding views over the Aire
Valley to Ovenden Moor, Earl Crag, Pendle Hill, Pinhaw, Bowland,
The Standard, Barden Moor and Great Whernside. With the views
to your right head on the road beneath White Crag as far as the
second house, White Crag. From a gate after it drop through an
enclosure and descend a couple of field centres through gates.
Then bear left to the bottom corner to drop to a gate onto a road.
From a stile a few strides left, cross to another wall-stile: grand
views look over the valley of Holden Beck. Advance on a field bottom
to a corner stile, then on the bank past springs before a gentle
slant down this broad pasture to a wall-stile opposite. Another is
seen ahead, from where slant down to an aqueduct on Holden Beck.

Descend to a footbridge and cobbled ford, and turn
downstream to a gate. A track rises away to swing sharp left uphill:
instead advance straight on a grassy way through gorse, crossing a
sidestream and on towards a wall. Ascend the wallside, slanting
directly up at a corner to follow a higher wall up to a gate. Through
this a grassy track heads away right. Quickly joining a firmer
track, double back left on this and as it climbs away, pass through
a fence-gate in front. A grassier track continues, winding down to
run above a wall through roughish pasture. Drawing level with a
small length of old wall it slants up to a gate in a fence. Don't rise
higher on it but bear off left to a ruinous barn, Out Laith. A wall-

stile in front sends you across a moist dip to another such stile at the old barn. Go straight ahead, down the bank to a slab bridge on Dirk Hill Sike. Just upstream is a stile, from where ascend the bank and cross to a gate/stile in the far corner where two walls meet.

Advance along the wallside until crossing it at a solid stile after the arrival of a track and before Far Ghyll Grange. Slant to a stile in the ascending wall to the left, then to a gate above. Head away with the wall to a stile in it, then make for the house at Black Pots, with a stile just in front. Turn left on its drive until it runs free above Doubler Stones Farm. Just before a bungalow turn up a path onto the moor beneath the charismatic, weirdly weathered Doubler Stones. Beyond a kissing-gate in a fence the path rises gently into heather to a wall-stile on the crest of Rombalds Moor. Just a minute further comes arrival at Windgate Nick, a memorable moment that brings Wharfedale spectacularly into the scene.

Beneath your feet old quarries fall away to the farms of Addingham Moorside. Beyond are Beamsley Beacon and Simon's Seat, with Barden Moor leading the eye to distant Buckden Pike and Great Whernside, while Rombalds Moor stretches far above Ilkley. Turn left along the escarpment path to rejoin the wall. As sunken ways turn downhill, remain on the path beneath the wall to a corner stile. Go left outside a plantation to Nab End, a final dramatic moment overlooking Lightbank Lane and the Airedale panorama. The path drops past minor rocks to a stile back to the start.

Doubler Stones

*3¹4 miles
from Holden Gate*

**Beautiful woodland and
beck scenery under the
moorland fringe between
Silsden and Riddlesden**

Start Lay-by (GR: 065442) just past Holden Gate, reached
from Riddlesden by Granby Lane, Banks Lane, Silsden Road
Map OS Explorer OL21, South Pennines (or 297)

From the start extensive views over the Aire Valley take
in Ovenden Moor, Nab Hill, Worth Valley, Earl Crag, Pendle Hill and
Pinhaw. At the lay-by a gate sends a bridleway angling away from
the road alongside a wall. This rises faintly to a corner on Pinfold
Hill, with small outcrops and outstanding views over Silsden and
South Craven, as far as the Bowland moors over Farnhill Pinnacle,
also rolling Dales heights of the Malhamdale Hills, Barden Moor and
Great Whernside. Continuing, slant left of the mast and a grassy
track runs to a gate in the wall ahead. A super green way continues
along the wallside to The Crag. Keep on above the buildings, merging
into a track that runs on through the farmyard and away. The side
valley of Holden Beck is now fully outspread in front.

Keep on until the track slants up to the right, where bear
left on a grassy track dropping to a gate in the wall below. Descend
the wallside, and approaching a gate at the bottom bear right to
drop down with a continuing wall. Towards the bottom bear right
between gorse bushes, and across a small sidestream a short green
way runs on to a firmer track. Go left on this towards a gate just
ahead, but before it, double back left on a path above the confines
of the beck. Entering its wooded environs at a stile, an absorbing
path meanders downstream in colourful surrounds: at an early fork
bear right dropping into much broader confines. A minute later you

pass a junction where you can double back down a flight of steps to peer into a mini-ravine secreting a waterfall. The splendid main path forges on beneath big boulders, rising out of the trees to merge with another path in a large pasture refreshed with young trees. This quickly merges into a track to a gate onto a sharp corner of Holden Lane. Turn down the road as far as a gate on the left, then cross a field bottom to experience the joys of Spring Crag Wood.

Within a minute take a fork left, a brief climb preceding a long, level stride through beautiful woodland. At the far end the path crosses a track to rise briefly to a wall-stile into a field. Slant gently up a grassy rake to a gate, then cross to another, now with big Airedale views again. Ignoring this gate go right above a spring to a corner stile. This sends a delightful path on through scattered woodland and bracken to emerge onto Riddlesden golf course. With sweeping views to Keighley and the Worth Valley, advance along the top. The path reforms to meander through colourful vegetation atop the course before reaching a stile in the corner. Cross a stream to a wall corner opposite, but approaching the corner ahead double back left up a thin path to a stile by the top corner, above a boulder. Maintain this line linked by wall-stiles across three fields to a gate back onto the road at Holden Gate, with the start just to the left.

Summer meadow above Spring Crag Wood

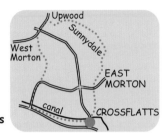

*4¹2 miles
from Crossflatts*

**Wooded Sunnydale is
a local gem, while the
return via West Morton
gives extensive open views**

*Start Morton Lane (GR: 099411), roadside parking
Map OS Explorer 297, Lower Wharfedale/Washburn Valley*

The village centre has the Royal pub, shops and a railway
station. Follow Morton Lane up to the Leeds-Liverpool Canal at
Morton Bridge. Cross the swing bridge and within yards take a stile
on the right. An enclosed path heads away, rising into trees then
slanting up a field. Fine views look to Micklethwaite across the side
valley of Morton Beck. At the top a wall leads along to a stile onto
an urban road on the edge of East Morton. Advance briefly to turn
right at a T-junction. Within yards turn up a cobbled drive on the
left, from where a snicket rises to emerge as Little Lane onto
Otley Road. Further left are the Busfeild Arms, Post office/shop
and WC. Cross with care and up a flight of steps to head along
Green End Road. Passed on the left is mullioned windowed Manor
Farm, while to the right is a large stone aqueduct.

Reaching a fork facing the grounds of Morton Hall, take
the rough Upwood Lane left. At a junction below a farm go right, a
good track heading away to rise through colourful surrounds to
wooded Sunnydale. As the track swings to cross the beck, advance
to the dam of Sunnydale Reservoir. Across, a path climbs the steep
bank to a junction. Turn left, initially muddy but transforming into
a superb woodland path. Passing the surprise of a small, colourful
dam, the path runs on the wood top to a corner where fallen trees
frame a waterfall on Sweet Well Dike. The path doubles back left
then right to trace the wood top to a gate at the end. This puts you

onto a cart track, which drops left over Bradup Beck and rises to approach Upwood Hall. Over to the right is a big sweep of Morton Moor beneath the masts at Whetstone Gate. Before the farm buildings turn sharp right to rise away to meet Ilkley Road.

Turn left to a crossroads with Street Lane. Descend past the chalets of Highbeck Park to a bend ahead and bear left down the drive to Moorside Cottages. Along the front a little path drops down to a stile into a field. Big views now look over the Aire Valley to Keighley and its Worth Valley skyline. Drop left to a stile and down again to a gate/stile in the bottom corner. Across a tiny enclosure stiles between buildings put you onto a driveway at the hamlet of West Morton. Advance to where the access road climbs away, then take a gate after it and resume across a field bottom above more dwellings. The path runs through several small pastures via wall-stiles to a corner one onto another access road at the end of the hamlet. Turn down this into the middle yard below, and down to a gate into a field. An enclosed path runs down its left side, becoming fully enclosed. After a moist level spell it turns to run downhill in fine style, enclosed by greenery all the way to emerge onto Carr Lane. Go right and down Swine Lane's roadside footway to reach the canal. Across the footbridge join the towpath, doubling back under the bridges and quickly returning to Morton Bridge.

Sunnydale

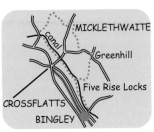

*3½ miles
from Bingley*

**Towpath and beckside lead
to a lovely old village,
though Five Rise Locks
remain the highlight**

Start Rail station (GR: 107391), car parks
Map OS Explorer 288, Bradford & Huddersfield

From the station turn right onto Park Road, and right
again over the dual carriageway. After crossing the parallel Leeds-
Liverpool Canal take a path left down onto its bank, and head away
past the Damart factory to reach Three Rise Locks. Cross by a swing
bridge at the top and resume on the towpath, revealing the Five
Rise Locks ahead, showpiece of the canal. Here for over 200 years,
five interlinking locks have lifted boats up a watery staircase - a
fascinating spectacle and a fine piece of engineering. At the top is
a café which you may enjoy on returning to this point. For now
advance on the towpath past colourful boats to Micklethwaite Wharf.

Cross Micklethwaite Lane and continue to a swing bridge
on Morton Lane. Cross and at once take a stile on the right, from
where a surfaced path heads away. Entering a few trees, take a
right fork to a footbridge on Morton Beck and resume upstream. A
stile into a field takes you outside the beck up to a stile onto a level
path. Go left, rejoining the beck to reach a delectable, tree-fringed
millpond, with the old chimney evident across it. Resuming, the mill-
cut is bridged and the beck leads to a bridge on it. Don't cross but
turn right on the enclosed ascending way, which quickly runs along
to a corner of Micklethwaite. Absorbing a track into housing, turn
right at the end and up onto the road through the village alongside
a chapel and opposite the delightful corner of High Fold. Further
down the street are Micklethwaite Grange (1695) and the Old Hall.

Go left a few strides to a steep, sloping green, whose 'summit' seats may well delay you. Leave by the hairpin bend on the right, where a level path heads away from a gate. At the end a drive leads on beneath a heather bank and above Fair Lady Farm to a stile at the end. A grand path heads away, soon becoming enclosed by walls to run a truly delightful, largely level course with views right to the Druid's Altar, and scattered bracken woodland above. At the end it emerges onto steeply climbing Greenhill Lane. Turn left up its footway to a junction with Lady Lane.

On the very junction take a bridle-gate on the right, and a firm path winds down through a sliver of woodland. This course is maintained for some time, remarkably so amid much encroaching suburbia. Ultimately it drops onto a street. Cross to Pinedale and descend to find a corner snicket sending you off again. Through further greenery this drops to a narrow access road. Look to the right to see the splendid late 16th century house of Gawthorpe Hall, well tucked away with some old cottages close by. From a stile and steps opposite descend to a kissing-gate onto a driveway which leads down onto a through road. Turn right above allotments, and at the end go left down Beck Lane to return to the top of the Five Rose Locks and possible refreshment. Retrace opening steps on the towpath back into Bingley.

Five Rise Locks

39

4 miles
from Bingley

Riverbank and richly
wooded surrounds
lead to a charismatic
Airedale viewpoint

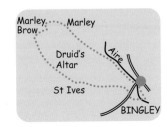

Marley
Brow ⋯⋯ Marley

Druid's
Altar

Aire

St Ives

BINGLEY

Start Parish church (GR: 106394), car parks nearby
Map OS Explorer 288, Bradford & Huddersfield

Bingley is a bustling town which has retained some older
corners, notably the environs of the parish church. In the spacious
park is the Georgian Town Hall, while nearby is the Market Hall. A
remarkable aspect of the town is that the river flowing parallel to
its busy main street has repelled any development on its western
bank. From the cobbled Old Main Street by the church, cross the
Aire by Ireland Bridge, linking the historic Old White Horse Inn
with the welcoming Brown Cow. Turn sharp right on Ireland Street,
quickly turning right again in front of a housing development. An
unsurfaced road heads upstream in tandem with the river, through
increasingly wooded surrounds. This access road later leaves the
river to run beneath wooded slopes to Raven Royd, a lovely old
house with arch-headed mullioned windows.

Pass to its right, on through the farmyard and along the
continuing drive to Cophurst. Pass left of the house and out into a
field. A cart track continues through the fields beneath a wooded
bank to merge into a track at the end. Advance to a gate, and a
grass track runs on to a stile onto an access road from the hamlet
of Marley. Over to the right is the impressive old Marley Hall. Go
left the few yards towards Blakey Cottage with its 1694 datestone
and turn up its near side on a steep driveway. This swings right of
a house above, to a gate. A track ascends increasingly colourful
Marley Brow to a lone house at Transfield Hole. All of this section
enjoys extensive Aire Valley views to the Rombalds Moor skyline.

An improving track continues up, eventually petering out. Rise to a kissing-gate from where a good path climbs through bracken. Near the top fork left to rise further before commencing a superb ramble along the crest of this moorland enclosure. With a wall above, the path runs delightfully through heather, bilberry and bracken terrain on Transfield Top, to ultimately emerge onto an access road. Cross over, and just a minute further is the Druid's Altar. Gritstone outcrops form a well-defined edge in colourful open country, the finest location from which to survey the view.

At the end of the rocks leave the edge on a path bearing right to unsurfaced Altar Lane. A gateway opposite accesses St Ives estate: bear left on the main bridleway, running a pleasant enclosed course down to swing sharply right at a barn. Here a short-cut drops left onto another walled way, running briefly left then forking to slant down to rejoin Altar Lane. Resume downhill, trees on the left quickly ending to reveal more views across the valley. Towards the bottom it swings right to meet the Harden road. Cross to a broad track dropping down into more trees, running along to emerge into an open pasture shrouded by greenery. Bear left to join the river and quickly reach and cross an iron footbridge into Myrtle Park. For the town centre go straight up, for Ireland Bridge turn left on the riverside walk. This pleasant little stroll clings to the river, and en route passes steps up onto Market Street, and the Ailsa Well.

At the Druid's Altar

41

*4¹4 miles
from St Ives*

**A brilliantly colourful
walk with richly
varied water and
woodland features**

Start **St Ives golf club (GR: 092390), public car park**
Map **OS Explorer 288, Bradford & Huddersfield**

St Ives estate is a fine mix of woodland, moorland and
farmland with golf course, riding centre and 19th century mansion.
Rejoin the main drive and turn right past the Coach House. Opposite
the tearoom enter a picnic area, going right on a path into trees.
Joining another bear right to pass beneath the drive, swinging
round to Coppice Pond. Bear left on the shoreline path, merging into
a broader one to continue beyond the lake. At a junction fork left
to drop through trees back onto the drive at St Ives Lodge. Exiting
onto Keighley Road drop left into Harden, with its Golden Fleece,
Post office and shop. From the staggered crossroads head along
Wilsden Road, descending to Harden Beck at the Malt Shovel pub.

Across the bridge bear right to climb the sidelined Mill
Hill Top. The main road is rejoined at a garden centre, from whose
entrance cross the road to a stile. A slim path descends to cross
Wilsden Beck, then crosses to a little gate into wooded Sandy
Banks. Don't join the broad track ahead but turn right up a wallside path. Meeting the track on a bend, bear right again on a path
rising gently to run through delightful bracken-floored woodland.
It later rises to join a wallside path. Bear right to become enclosed
at a stile, with Wilsden outspread. After just a few strides take a
gap-stile on the left, and head away with a wall through several
fields to join Lee Lane. Over to the left is the St Ives estate, with
Baildon Moor straight ahead. Between the two is Rombalds Moor.

Go left 25 yards to a stile on the right, and head away with the wall. In the corner an enclosed way curves between fields: emerging, bear right to a stile near the far corner, and cross a last field to a corner stile into trees at Black Hills. A good path drops through the wood, merging into a broader way to run briefly right. The path soon turns down the slope as a stonier, sunken way before again running right to a stile out of the trees. Slant right through low outcrops: this lovely pasture is surrounded by greenery, with the St Ives estate across Harden Beck. A stile on the right sees you onto a golf course: bear left down it guided by a series of white painted rocks. When they end, go left across a fairway towards a former mill. Leaving the course it becomes enclosed to bridge Harden Beck, emerging alongside the mill onto Beck Foot Lane. Go briefly right on this rough road to Beck Foot, an idyllic location with an 18th century arched bridge, ford and desirable cottages.

Don't cross the bridge but take a stile on the left and head on through the field above the River Aire. Rising to a solitary house, don't enter the trees but go left past the garden to join the short drive onto Beck Foot Lane. Ascend to the Bingley road, crossing to a path slanting left up through the woods of St Ives to emerge onto the main drive. From the car park entrance just above, a path climbs into trees then runs left to a junction at a witch sculpture. A short path rises right to a gate into a new wood. At the far end is a gate onto the enclosed track of Blind Lane. Turn uphill to join a broad track. Go left on this, soon dropping down to finish.

The Aire at Beckfoot

4 miles
from Eldwick

**A gentle approach to a
hugely popular playground,
with colourful surrounds
and intriguing history too**

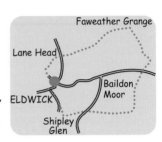

Start Acorn Inn (GR: 125406), roadside parking
Map OS Explorer 288, Bradford & Huddersfield

Head up the side road of The Green past the pub, an
access road running on to double back right to a cottage, then
swing left to the Old Corn Mill. Don't enter but cross the stream
on the right and an enclosed path ascends to a stile into a field.
Baildon Moor looks a long way over to the right! Rise with the wall
to a gate/stile, and up again to a snicket in the top corner between
gardens to the cluster of houses at Lane Head. Emerging into the
yard, go right on a short enclosed path to join a short drive onto a
road. A little further left, and well seen from the roadside is the
splendid old house of Eldwick Hall , with its 1696 datestone.

Just a few yards left, however, take a grassy walled
track right. Emerging into a field the way continues to a gate, and
on to a path crossroads at a wall corner. Go straight on to a wall-
stile ahead. Cross a horse track into unkempt pasture and advance
on a fading trod over improving grassy terrain, contouring straight
on to meet the horse track again. Now continue on with it as Birch
Close Lane: equestrian use has obliterated this ancient moorland
packway. Approaching Birch Close it forks: go left a few yards then
escape right on a grassy walled way to the house. Go straight ahead
on the drive, when it swings left keep on a walled access track down
to Faweather Farm. At a junction at the bottom go right on Sconce
Lane. On your left is Faweather Grange, a small grange of Rievaulx
Abbey, whose monks mined ironstone nearby.

Keep straight on this rough lane until dropping to a large building in trees. A gap-stile takes you past it to another stile onto the foot of Baildon Moor. From a cross-paths in front, go straight up the little path winding delightfully through heather, bilberry and bracken. Meeting a grass track near the top, bear right up over a fairway to a parking area on the moor road. Cross onto a broad path, quickly forking left to rise to a brow revealing the OS column on Baildon Hill ahead. Advance to this on a gentle rise, crossing Dobrudden farm road. The panorama reaches far beyond Bradford, along the Pennine crest to Keighley and over Bingley Moor. Leave by bearing right to a path dropping towards Dobrudden caravan site. Just to your right are the curious tor-like 'cinder caves': for many centuries the moor was mined for coal, and these are slagheaps.

The path re-crosses the access road to the site corner, then along its wall to a corner overlooking Shipley Glen. Take the direct path dropping through bracken to meet the open road at the same point as an access road. Cross straight over and down through further bracken, retaining the main path's direct descent with the wooded moor edge to your right. Lower down it squeezes between recolonised quarries and the beck, dropping onto a broad track in front of a bridge on Loadpit Beck. Cross it and head away on the narrow lane, rising to absorb further lanes, with the wooded beck still to your right. Re-entering Eldwick at its war memorial, cross to the footway and the start is one minute down to the right.

Faweather Grange

*4¹4 miles
from Saltaire*

**Two colourful waterways
lead to beautiful woodland
and gritstone outcrops at a
classic Yorkshire landmark**

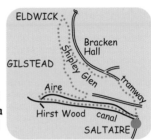

Start Rail station (GR: 139380), parking nearby
Map OS Explorer 288, Bradford & Huddersfield

Saltaire was a mill village created by Titus Salt, who moved his workers here from Bradford's polluted slums. From 1850 to 1872 hundreds of terraced dwellings were built to house the workforce of his worsted processing mill, an outstanding piece of industrial architecture 550-feet long and six storeys high. The village's grid system remains virtually intact, along with hospital, almshouses, schools and institute, and in 2001 was designated a World Heritage Site. From the station turn down Victoria Road, passing Salt's finest building: the Congregational Church was built in 1859 in rich Italian style, with a semicircular front and ornate circular tower.

After bridging the Leeds-Liverpool Canal, join and follow the towpath away. Beyond Hirst Wood Lock, enjoy Hirst Wood's greenery during a lovely stroll to an aqueduct over the River Aire, which has been parallel for some time. Immediately across take a stile on the right and a splendid path doubles back downstream with the river, clinging to its bank through deep foliage. Reaching a weir at Hirst Mill, leave the river on the driveway rising up onto a carriageway. Go left on a gentle slant between hedgerows up to a lodge. Go right up a continuing rougher enclosed track that ascends to an old iron kissing-gate onto a bridle-track with cobbled central strip. Engulfed in woodland rise up on this, emerging at the top where it broadens and loses the cobbles. Here take a stile on the right and up the side of a paddock to an old house.

Bear right between garages to a small iron gate back into woodland, and just a few strides further a broad path is met. Now on the edge of Shipley Glen turn left, and remain on this grand path through oak woodland high above Loadpit Beck. Ultimately as the ravine becomes shallower the path forks: as the left branch rises to join Lode Pit Lane, your way slants down to a stone-arched bridge on the beck. Cross this and follow the main path doubling back right up the heathery bank, now on the open country of Shipley Glen proper. This rises to a road, but avoids it by continuing across the open grass, along the crest of a broken gritstone edge that forms above the wooded bank. This avoids traffic but not people, and leads along the full length of the glen. Shipley Glen has been a place of public resort since people first escaped city grime for weekend fresh air. The roadside Bracken Hall is a countryside centre with exhibitions and displays on local history and wildlife. Just before it is part of a Bronze Age circle with at least 60 stones still in place.

Remain on open ground all the way to the Old Glen House pub and tearooms at the far end. Continue along suburban Prod Lane to Shipley Glen Cable Tramway: built in 1895, its open cars convey visitors up the wooded bank to the glen. To its right a surfaced path descends Trench Wood to the bottom station, and runs on to join Higher Coach Road. Virtually opposite is an entrance to Roberts Park, the quickest finish going left around it edge to a large metal footbridge on the Aire, with the start just up above.

Shipley Glen

HILLSIDE GUIDES... cover much of Northern England

Other colour *Pocket Walks* guides (available now or shortly)
·UPPER WHARFEDALE ·MALHAMDALE ·NIDDERDALE
·AIRE VALLEY ·HARROGATE & KNARESBOROUGH
·AMBLESIDE & LANGDALE ·BORROWDALE ·BOWLAND

Our *Walking Country* range features more great walks...

·WHARFEDALE ·MALHAMDALE ·WENSLEYDALE
·HARROGATE & the WHARFE VALLEY ·SWALEDALE
·RIPON & LOWER WENSLEYDALE ·NIDDERDALE
·THREE PEAKS ·HOWGILL FELLS
·TEESDALE ·EDEN VALLEY ·ALSTON & ALLENDALE

·NORTH YORK MOORS, SOUTH ·HOWARDIAN HILLS

·ILKLEY MOOR ·BRONTE COUNTRY ·CALDERDALE
·PENDLE & the RIBBLE ·WEST PENNINE MOORS
·ARNSIDE & SILVERDALE ·LUNESDALE ·BOWLAND

·LAKELAND FELLS, SOUTH ·LAKELAND FELLS, EAST
·LAKELAND FELLS, NORTH ·LAKELAND FELLS, WEST

Long Distance Walks, including
·COAST TO COAST WALK ·CUMBRIA WAY ·DALES WAY
·LADY ANNE'S WAY ·BRONTE WAY ·NIDDERDALE WAY
·WESTMORLAND WAY ·FURNESS WAY ·PENDLE WAY

Also available
·YORKSHIRE DALES, MOORS & FELLS
·THE HIGH PEAKS OF ENGLAND & WALES

Visit www.hillsidepublications.co.uk
or write for a catalogue